Hungry sharks c[...] other **prey**, whi[...] crabs scuttle along the sandy ocean floor.

Crab

Shark

Let's find out what happens in this habitat. Welcome to the ocean!

Earth's Vast Oceans

A blue whale slowly swims to the surface of the ocean.

It is the largest animal on Earth, and its watery home is Earth's largest habitat.

Blue whale

Scientists on a boat

Blue whales live in all of Earth's oceans, except in the Arctic.

Arctic Ocean

Atlantic Ocean

Pacific Ocean

Indian Ocean

Southern Ocean

Blue whales usually swim alone or in small groups.

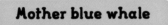
Calf

Mother blue whale

Some of them **migrate**, or move, to warm water to **mate** and give birth.

Then they swim back to colder waters to feed.

A newborn blue whale calf is 26 feet (8 m) long. It grows quickly, feeding on its mother's rich, fatty milk for up to eight months.

What do you think this enormous whale eats?

Life at the Top

Krill are small, shrimp-like animals.

At night they swim to the water's surface in swarms to feed.

Krill

Bioluminescence

Plankton

Krill are almost see-through, but they are easy to spot at night. They have special body parts that give off light, called bioluminescence.

They eat microscopic plants, called phytoplankton, and microscopic animals, called zooplankton.

A blue whale is waiting, and krill are its main food.

The whale rushes at the swarm, opens its huge mouth, and fills it with water and 500,000 krill!

Swarm of krill

Blue whale

The water filters out through **baleen plates** in the whale's mouth. But the tasty krill are trapped.

Baleen plate

Who else might enjoy a meal of krill?

Hungry Hunters

A crabeater seal dives into the cold Southern Ocean.

You might think this seal eats crabs, but its main food is krill.

Crabeater seal

Crabeater seals have special sieve-like teeth that act like the blue whale's baleen plates.

Teeth

Crabeater seal skull

Crabeater seal

Orca

A group of orcas spot the crabeater seal as he clambers onto a chunk of ice.

The orcas swim toward the ice, making a wave to knock the seal back into the water!

The seal clings on, and the hungry hunters swim away.

What plant-like living thing is growing in the ocean?

An Underwater Forest

Kelp gull

Kelp forest

Seal

The hungry kelp gull lands on a floating mat of plant-like **algae**, called kelp.

Insects and maggots that live on the kelp are tasty treats for the gull.

Fish hide from **predators**, such as sharks, in the kelp. Seals come to the forest to have their babies.

The kelp clings to the seabed and forms a thick underwater forest.

Sea otters wrap their bodies in kelp to anchor themselves in rough Pacific seas.

The kelp helps the otters, and the otters help protect the kelp by eating sea urchins.

Sea otter

Kelp

Sea urchin

Sea urchins are small seabed animals that feed on the roots, or holdfasts, of kelp.

If kelp loses its roots, it dies.

The decorator crab is a master of disguise. How did it get its name?

Hiding on the Seabed

Hardly any predators eat the decorator crab.
That's because they can't find it!

Decorator crab

These crabs decorate themselves with seaweed, coral,
and rocks from their seabed home.

They even use small animals, such as sea anemones.

14

The crabs fasten their decorations to hooked bristles on their shells.

This **camouflage** helps protect the crabs from predators.

Sea anemone

Decorator crab

Decorator crabs eat plankton and dead animals. Luckily for the anemones attached to their bodies, the crabs are messy eaters. The anemones eat the crab's floating leftovers.

What do you think the ocean is like in its deepest parts?

Deep-Sea Life

No sunlight reaches the deepest parts of the ocean, and the water is very cold.

Some animals create their own light, called bioluminescence.

The anglerfish uses its glowing lure to attract prey.

Lure

Anglerfish

Food such as whale poop and rotting dead animals floats down from above.

This food is called marine snow.

Whale poop

Vampire squid

Filament

A vampire squid catches marine snow with two long, sticky parts called filaments.

Sometimes a huge feast falls from above. What could it be?

A Feast Arrives!

When a whale dies, its body sinks to the ocean floor.

This is known as a "whale fall," and it can feed many animals for up to 50 years.

Sharks, hagfish, and other animals tear the whale apart, feeding on its meat.

Whale fall

Octopus

Octopuses, eels, sea cucumbers, clams, and other animals also join the feast.

After about 10 years, all that's left are bones.

Hagfish

Bone-eating worms tunnel into the bones to feed on fats and oil. Nothing goes to waste!

Sea cucumber

Clams

Bone-eating worm

Which of these animals has eight legs and makes a den in an underwater rock?

Amazing Octopus

An octopus squeezes into a crack in a rock to hide.

The crack will be her den where she lays thousands of eggs.

Octopus

When an octopus wants to hide from predators, special **cells** in its body can change color to match the rock around it.

An octopus's eggs can take a year to hatch.

The octopus guards her eggs and does not eat.

Shortly after the babies hatch, the mother octopus dies.

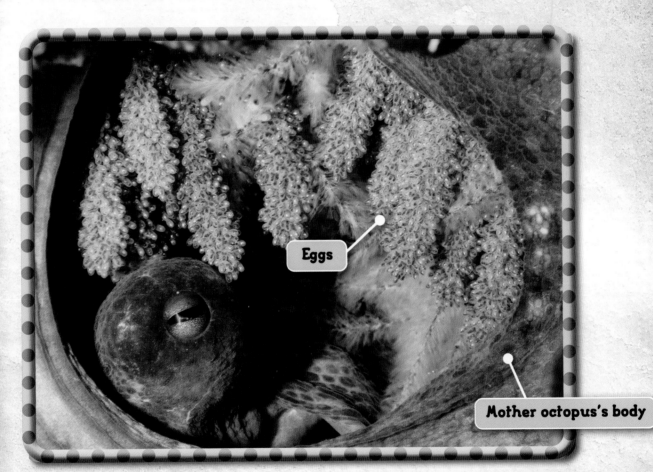

Eggs

Mother octopus's body

What do the baby octopuses become once they hatch?

Safety in Numbers

The tiny baby octopuses become zooplankton.

They are too small to swim, so they get washed into clouds of plankton.

Some of them become food for whales, krill, or a shoal of hungry mackerel.

Baby octopus hatching

Octopus eggs

22

Mackerel travel together for safety and for hunting smaller fish.

When under attack, mackerel form a bait ball.

It's difficult for predators to spot and grab a single fish from the fast-moving ball.

A mackerel bait ball

A female mackerel may lay 500,000 tiny eggs at one time. Other fish feed on the floating eggs. Hungry mackerel may even eat their own eggs!

What hungry hunters are speeding toward the mackerel?

Gone Fishing!

The orcas are still hungry.

They send out clicking sounds as they swim.

Orca

The sounds bounce off a bait ball of fish and echo back.

The orcas move in, slapping the fish with their tails to stun them.

A group of orcas may even hunt a blue whale. They surround it, chase it, and bite it until it becomes too weak to escape.

Two pelicans dive into a bait ball, opening their large bills.

Water flows out of the birds' bills, leaving fish caught in their pouches.

Pelican

Bill

Pouch

Pelican

Can you guess which animal is one of the ocean's top predators?

The Great White Shark

Adult great white sharks eat seals and sealions. They are the top predators in their ocean habitat.

They are expert hunters with streamlined bodies, powerful tails, and 300 sharp teeth.

Great white shark

Baby great white sharks hatch from eggs inside their mother's body.

After hatching, pups may feed on the unhatched eggs of their brothers and sisters!

The pups keep growing inside their mother and are 5 feet (1.5 m) long when they are born.

Newborn great white shark pups quickly swim away from their mother as she might think that they are prey!

Scientists checking a great white shark pup

Which small fish isn't scared of sharks?

The Shark Cleaner

Remoras are fish that attach themselves to the underside of sharks using suction cups on the tops of their heads. Why?

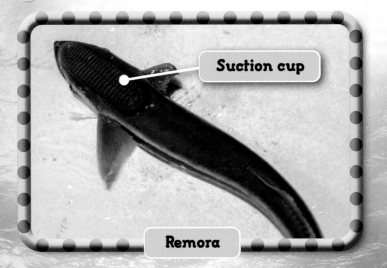

Suction cup

Remora

Lemon shark

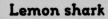

Remora fish

The fish eat the food scraps that the sharks drop.

The remoras also get protection from predators and free transportation!

In return, the fish eat **parasites** from the shark's skin, mouth, and even its nostrils.

A partnership between two different animals that helps them both is called a symbiotic relationship. Sharks will sometimes slow down to allow a remora to hitch a ride.

Lemon shark

Remora fish

Every living thing in the ocean relies on its habitat and its neighbors for survival.

An Ocean Food Web

A food web shows who eats who in a habitat.

This food web shows the connections between some of the living things in the ocean.

Plants and algae can make the food they need for energy inside themselves. To do this, they need sunlight.

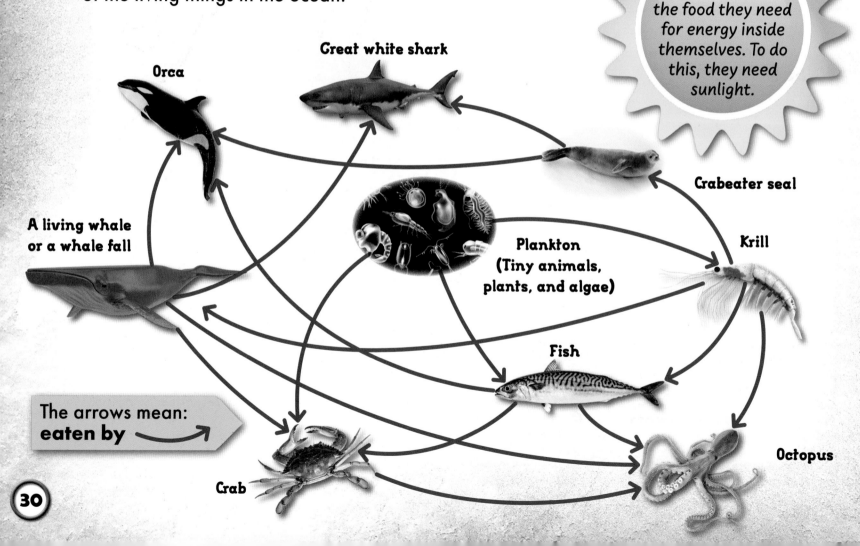

Orca

Great white shark

Crabeater seal

A living whale or a whale fall

Plankton (Tiny animals, plants, and algae)

Krill

Fish

The arrows mean: **eaten by**

Crab

Octopus

Glossary

algae
Plant-like living things that mostly grow and live in water. Like plants, algae use sunlight to make their own food.

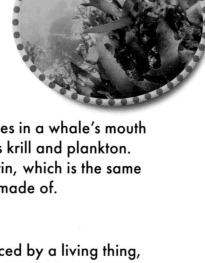

baleen plates
Fringe-like sheets of bristles in a whale's mouth that trap tiny food such as krill and plankton. They are made from keratin, which is the same stuff your fingernails are made of.

bioluminescence
Natural light that's produced by a living thing, such as some insects, fish, and krill.

camouflage
Colors, markings, or body parts that help an animal blend into its habitat.

cell
A very tiny part of a living thing.

habitat
The place where a living thing, such as a plant or animal, makes its home. The ocean, forests, and gardens are all types of habitats.

mate
To get together to produce young.

migrate
To move from one place to another. For example, animals migrate to find food or mates.

parasite
A living thing that lives on another living thing and may cause it harm.

predator
An animal that hunts and eats other animals.

prey
An animal that is hunted by other animals for food.

Published in 2024 by Ruby Tuesday Books Ltd.

Editor: Ruth Owen
Design and Production: Alix Wood

Photo credits
Alamy: 10B (Panther Media); 14 (Blue Planet Archive); Ardea: 17B (Steve Downer); NOAA: 18; Nature Picture Library: 6 (Flip Nicklin); 7 (Mark Carwardine); 9T (Richard Herrmann); 9B (Frank Lane Picture Agency); 12R (Brandon Cole); 13T (Tom Mangelsen); 16 (David Shale); 22 (Norbert Wu); 23 (Franco Banfi); 24 (Tony Wu); 28 (Ralph Pace); 29 (Pascal Kobeh); Public Domain: 19T; Gregory Rouse: 19BL; Shutterstock: Cover (Fotokon); 2–3; 4T (Neil Bromhall); 4B (Henner Damke); 5T (pablopicasso); 5B (Maui Topical Images); 10 (Mariusz Potocki); 11T (Vlad Silver); 11B (Doug Allan); 12L (Sergey Uryadnikov); 13B (Yvonne89); 17T (wildestanimal); 19BR (Porco Rosso); 20 (Dario Sabljak); 21 (scubadesign); 25 (retofuerst); 25B (Brian Lasenby); 26 (Martin Prochazkacz); 28L (Fiona Ayerst); 28R (Andrea Izzotti); 30–31; Superstock: 8 (Photoshot); 15 (Andrey Nekrasov).

Library of Congress Control Number: 2023902807
Print (Hardback) ISBN 978-1-78856-291-1
Print (Paperback) ISBN 978-1-78856-292-8
eBook PDF ISBN 978-1-78856-293-5
ePub ISBN 978-1-78856-294-2

Published in Minneapolis, MN
Printed in the United States

www.rubytuesdaybooks.com

Contents

Words shown in **bold** in the text are explained in the glossary.

Welcome to the Ocean

Who and what lives in Earth's oceans?

These huge areas of water are home to many different types of living things.

The plants and animals in an ocean get what they need to live from their **habitat**.

Anglerfish

Octopus

An ocean is a type of ecosystem. An ecosystem includes all the living things in an area. It also includes non-living things such as water, rocks, sand, and sunlight. Everything in an ecosystem has its own part to play.